Leaving My Homeland

A Refugee's Journey from

Colombia

Linda Barghoorn

Crabtree Publishing Company

www.crabtreebooks.com

Crabtree Publishing Company
www.crabtreebooks.com

Author: Linda Barghoorn

Editors: Sarah Eason, Harriet McGregor, and Janine Deschenes

Proofreader and indexer: Wendy Scavuzzo

Editorial director: Kathy Middleton

Design: Jessica Moon

Cover design and additional artwork: Jessica Moon

Photo research: Rachel Blount

Production coordinator and Prepress technician: Ken Wright

Print coordinator: Margaret Amy Salter

Consultants: Hawa Sabriye and HaEun Kim

Produced for Crabtree Publishing Company by Calcium Creative.

Publisher's Note: The story presented in this book is a fictional account based on extensive research of real-life accounts by refugees, with the aim of reflecting the true experience of refugee children and their families.

Photo Credits:

t=Top, bl=Bottom Left, br=Bottom Right

Shutterstock: Eduardo Accorinti: p. 15; F. A. Alba: p. 26; Rafal Cichawa: p. 19; Creative Photo Corner: p. 5b; De Visu: p. 25; Fotos593: pp. 7, 11, 20; Filipe Frazao: p. 14; Free Wind 2014: p. 10; Ivan_Sabo: p. 9; Jess Kraft: p. 17; Macrovector: p. 3; Svetlana Maslova: p. 29b; Andres Navia Paz: p. 6; Phipatbig: p. 11t; Matyas Rehak: pp. 13, 21; Seita: p. 1b; Svinkin: p. 1b; Mascha Tace: pp. 10–11 c; Barna Tanko: pp. 4, 12; Andres Virviescas: p. 8; What's My Name: p. 19t; UNHCR: © UNHCR/Luis Eduardo Parada Contreras: p. 23; © UNHCR/Magui Masseroni: p. 22; © UNHCR/Santiago Arcos Veintimilla: p. 24; Wikimedia Commons: Wilson Dias: p. 27.

Cover: Shutterstock: Macrovector.

Library and Archives Canada Cataloguing in Publication

Barghoorn, Linda, author
     A refugee's journey from Colombia / Linda Barghoorn.

(Leaving my homeland)
Includes index
Issued in print and electronic formats.
ISBN 978-0-7787-3672-1 (hardcover).--
ISBN 978-0-7787-3678-3 (softcover).--ISBN 978-1-4271-1969-8 (HTML)

     1. Refugees--Colombia--Juvenile literature. 2. Refugees--Ecuador--Juvenile literature. 3. Refugee children--Colombia--Juvenile literature. 4. Refugee children--Ecuador--Juvenile literature. 5. Refugees--Social conditions--Juvenile literature. 6. Colombia--Social conditions--Juvenile literature. I. Title.

HV640.5.C7B37 2017   j305.9'0691409861   C2017-903555-X
                                                                   C2017-903556-8

Library of Congress Cataloging-in-Publication Data

CIP available at the Library of Congress

Crabtree Publishing Company
www.crabtreebooks.com   1-800-387-7650

Printed in Canada/092017/PB20170719

Published in Canada
Crabtree Publishing
616 Welland Ave.
St. Catharines, Ontario
L2M 5V6

Published in the United States
Crabtree Publishing
PMB 59051
350 Fifth Avenue, 59th Floor
New York, New York 10118

Published in the United Kingdom
Crabtree Publishing
Maritime House
Basin Road North, Hove
BN41 1WR

Published in Australia
Crabtree Publishing
3 Charles Street
Coburg North
VIC, 3058

What Is in This Book?

Leaving Colombia

Colombia has suffered through a **civil war** for more than 50 years. It began with an argument between farmers, wealthy landowners, and the government. The farmers were very poor. They wanted the landowners and government to give them better land rights. Rights are privileges and freedoms that are protected by laws. Their demands were refused. The farmers began fighting against the government. This grew into a fierce battle across Colombia.

This Colombian home lies empty and abandoned.

UN Rights of the Child

Every child has rights. **Refugees** have the right to special protection and help. The **United Nations (UN)** Convention on the Rights of the Child is a document that lists the rights that all children should have. Think about these rights as you read this book.

Thousands of Colombians fled to other countries to escape the fighting. These people are called refugees. Refugees flee their **homeland** because of war and other unsafe conditions. Refugees are different from **immigrants**. Immigrants choose to leave to look for better opportunities in another country.

Nicaragua

Caribbean Sea

Costa Rica

Panama

Venezuela

North
Pacific
Ocean

Bogotá

Colombia

Brazil

Ecuador

Colombia is at the northern tip
of South America. Bogotá is its
capital city.

Peru

The Colombian flag is
yellow, blue, and red. Yellow
represents the country's rich
resources; blue for the seas;
and red for the blood that has
been spilled during its war.

Many other Colombians fled
their homes and took shelter
in the forest, or in other cities
in Colombia. People who flee
their homes, but stay in their
country are called **internally
displaced persons (IDPs)**. Around
7.3 million IDPs live in Colombia.

5

My Homeland, Colombia

Spanish explorers reached South America in 1499. They settled the land that would become Colombia and named it after Christopher Columbus—although he never went there! Colombia has borders with Venezuela, Brazil, Peru, Ecuador, and Panama. It is a beautiful country with many different landscapes, such as mountains, volcanoes, grasslands, and tropical beaches.

Bogotá

Around 9.8 million people live in Bogotá.

Colombia is one of the world's largest coffee producers. Coffee is mostly grown in the mountains.

Colombia has a population of

47 million people.

Bolívar Square is a beautiful square in Bogotá. It is named after Simon Bolívar, a military leader who helped Colombia gain independence from Spain.

More than half of Colombia was once covered in rain forests. These forests are under attack because the land is being cleared for farming.

Colombia became **independent** from Spain in 1819. It is South America's oldest **democracy**. In a democracy, every citizen should have the same rights. Wealthy landowners ran the country's huge coffee plantations. The farmers who worked for them were treated like slaves and paid poorly. When the farmers demanded more rights and freedoms, they were ignored.

Andres's Story: Life in Colombia

I was born in a small village outside the city of Pasto, in western Colombia. My favorite part about living in Pasto was the lively Carnaval de Negros y Blancos (Carnival of the Blacks and Whites) that happens in January. A long time ago, this celebration honored the Moon Goddess who protected the crops. Now, it is a big party. Every year, our family enjoyed the celebrations. People made giant figures. They paraded the figures through the streets. We feasted on grilled cuy (guinea pig), a delicious local dish.

This is one of the giant floats created for the colorful Carnaval de Negros y Blancos in Pasto.

Colombia's Story in Numbers

In Colombia,

99 percent

of the people speak Spanish—the country's official language.

Soccer is Colombia's most popular sport.

I lived in a small farmhouse with my parents, three brothers, and one sister. Papá was a farmer who raised pigs and cows. Mamá took care of our family. She had a small vegetable garden where she grew a lot of our food.

We use corn in many of our foods. Arepa is a pancake-like bread made from corn flour. We eat it almost every day for breakfast. Mamá makes tamales often. They are a food made from corn dough and stuffed with meat or vegetables, then wrapped in a banana leaf.

I used to walk to school in our village each morning with my brothers and sister. After school, I liked to play soccer with my friends, Mateo and Sebastian, in the street near my house. I dreamed of being a professional player. We are crazy about soccer in my country!

War in Colombia

When the government refused to listen to the farmers' demands, some farmers formed groups of soldiers, known as **guerillas**. They fought the government for the rights of the poor. Soon, there was a civil war.

More guerrilla groups formed. They fought one another for power. The largest group was the Revolutionary Armed Forces of Colombia (FARC). At first, FARC fought for the rights of the farmers. However, as it gained power, FARC wanted to control Colombia. It organized **drug** cartels. These are groups that control the sale of illegal drugs. FARC's drug cartels sold drugs for money to buy more weapons.

Government soldiers search for FARC members.

The landowners formed paramilitary groups to protect themselves against FARC. A paramilitary group is a group of people who fight similar to an army.

Even Colombians living in remote regions have been forced from their homes because of war.

The war became more violent and dangerous. Many families were hurt or killed in the fighting. Often, they had to find protection from **rebel** groups. But the rebels often threatened people with violence in exchange for their support. Everyone was afraid of the guerilla and paramilitary soldiers.

Andres's Story: Living with Conflict

The war in Colombia started years before I was born. But it did not come to our village until I was nine years old. One day, a group of paras (paramilitary soldiers) arrived in our village. They threatened the families there, and demanded money from them. They said Papá had to give them a cow as payment to protect us from the FARC soldiers. Papá gave the paras a cow, hoping that would be the end of our troubles.

Children were often **recruited** or kidnapped by FARC from poor villages.

When the FARC soldiers came, they pretended to be friends with us. They showed me their guns and played games. But they began to threaten our family, too. When Papá complained to the police, they did nothing. The police were also afraid of FARC.

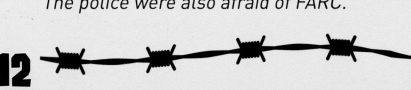

Colombia's Story in Numbers

Around
340,000
Colombian refugees live in Ecuador, Venezuela, Panama, and Costa Rica.

The fighting between FARC and the paras came closer. We heard the pop, pop, pop of gunfire nearby. One night, a bomb exploded and woke us all up. The next day, the FARC soldiers came to take my 15-year-old brother Diego to join their forces. When Mamá tried to stop them, they pointed their guns at us and threatened to kill us. They said Diego must help them protect us from the paras.

The paras began to make threats against our farm. They said we were supporting their enemy, FARC. Afraid for our lives, my parents decided we must leave. We left the village, our farm, our animals, and Mamá's lovely vegetable garden. We all cried, wondering where Diego had gone.

When people flee their homes, they leave behind everything they know and love.

Child Soldiers

Children are very **vulnerable** during wartime. Often, their families struggle to provide them with a safe home, food, and security. Guerilla groups in Colombia promised children food, clothing, and protection from the violence. They tried to convince children to leave their families and become child soldiers. Sometimes, families were forced to give one of their children to FARC in exchange for protection against other guerilla groups.

Often, child soldiers ran errands, carried bombs, or took part in attacks on villages. They were called "little bees" because they performed many tasks like worker bees. Both boys and girls were recruited. Some were as young as 10 years old.

Children have the right to live safe lives, but between 6,000 and 7,000 children have been forced to become child soldiers in Colombia.

UN Rights of the Child

Every child has the right to be protected from **exploitation**.

The child soldiers were poorly trained to fight in war. Many were killed. Some children tried to escape. Those who returned to their families often felt guilty and afraid. They could not forget the terrible things they had been forced to do. It would take them a long time to adjust to normal life again.

Some child soldiers were convinced that they were fighting an honorable war for their country. This made it easy for their commanders to control them, and turn them into violent and dangerous soldiers.

Children from poor families were often targeted for recruitment because the guerilla groups gave them false promises of a better life.

Andres's Story: Escaping to Bogotá

Papá drove all night. We stopped only to stretch our legs and go to the toilet. All we had to eat were the tamales Mamá had packed. It was cramped and uncomfortable in the truck. Late the next afternoon, we reached Bogotá. The city seemed big and scary.

Our route from Pasto to Bogotá.

Papá had to find us somewhere to live. He sold our old truck in exchange for a two-room shack in an area called Soacha, outside the city. Mamá tried to make it comfortable. But it was always dusty from the sand **quarry** nearby. The walls were cracked. It had no running water or a toilet.

Papá did not have any land to farm. So he had to look for another job. Some days, he could work in the quarry. Papá's face always looked worried when he had no work.

Soacha was a dangerous place. The police often raided our neighborhood. They arrested criminals and gang members. Once, they killed three boys from a family we knew. They claimed the boys were FARC rebels, but we knew that was not true. The police just wanted to collect reward money from the government for hunting down FARC members.

One day, the police set fire to our home. They said it was built illegally and that we were not allowed to live there. We escaped the fire. But now we had no house, no truck, no animals, and no garden.

Since 1990, the population of Soacha has grown from 250,000 to more than 550,000. Most of the new arrivals are IDPs.

What Paths Do Refugees Take?

Millions of Colombians fled their homes to escape the war. Some went to countries such as Ecuador, Venezuela, Panama, and Costa Rica.

Often they had no identity papers with them. Identity papers are an official record of who you are and where you have come from. Without these papers, they could not be official refugees. This means that they had no rights to government help, such as health care, education, housing, or other aid, in their **host country**. Many were immediately sent back to Colombia.

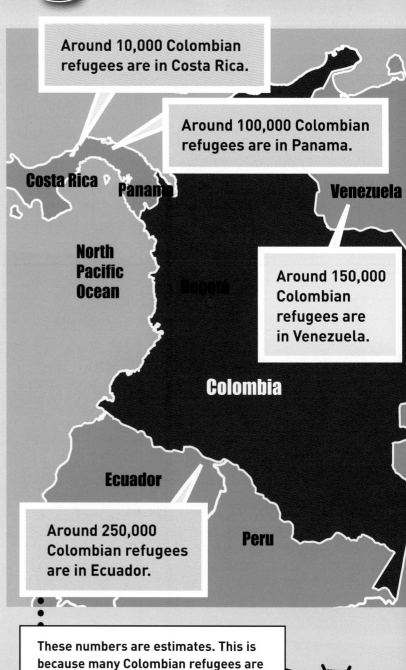

Around 10,000 Colombian refugees are in Costa Rica.

Around 100,000 Colombian refugees are in Panama.

Around 150,000 Colombian refugees are in Venezuela.

Around 250,000 Colombian refugees are in Ecuador.

Costa Rica
Panama
Venezuela
North Pacific Ocean
Bogotá
Colombia
Ecuador
Peru

These numbers are estimates. This is because many Colombian refugees are not officially registered as refugees.

Every child has the right to an identity. No one should take this right away from you.

Some refugees hid in the jungle to avoid being returned to Colombia.

Many fled to neighboring countries, but did not register as refugees. They were afraid of being sent home, and tried to hide in the jungles and cities. This made it hard to count how many Colombian refugees there were. Other Colombians became IDPs. They hid in remote areas or fled to the cities, where they lived in **slums**.

Most Colombian refugees and IDPs had to take care of themselves. There were no refugee camps to protect them. They did not receive help from the government in Colombia or host countries. They tried to avoid **discrimination** in their host country or violence in their home country.

Andres's Story: Flight to Ecuador

My papá decided we should leave Colombia and go to Ecuador. He said that we could start over there. He had heard that we could get help in a city called Ibarra. Mamá did not want to leave Colombia without Diego. But we did not know where to look for him.

We bought tickets and boarded the crowded bus. The bus ride took two days. It stopped at many different cities along the way. We only had a little food and water to share between us.

Colombian refugees do not pass through border crossings into Ecuador. They are afraid of being sent back to Colombia.

Only

1 in 3

Colombian refugees is allowed to settle in Ecuador.

Some Colombian refugees have settled in Ibarra, a city in northern Ecuador.

Papá was worried we would not be allowed to enter Ecuador. So we got off the bus at Ipiales. It was the last town in Colombia before the border. We started to walk. We walked through the forest until we came to a wide river. We walked several miles to find a footbridge to cross it. I was so afraid that we were lost. When we reached a town called Tulcán, we saw the flag of Ecuador flying from a building. We were safe in Ecuador!

In Tulcán, we boarded another bus to Ibarra. It was late when we arrived there. We slept at the bus terminal. The next day, we went to the **United Nations High Commissioner for Refugees (UNHCR)** office. After we showed them our identity papers, they welcomed us and gave us refugee identity cards. This meant that we were officially refugees, and allowed to stay in Ecuador.

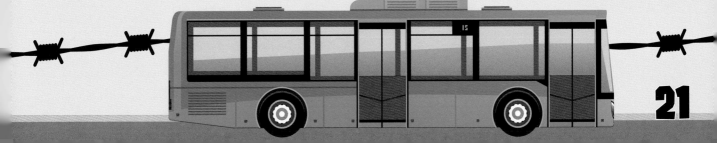

Challenges Refugees Face

Refugees often face discrimination and uncertainty. Many people in host countries did not trust the Colombian refugees. They were afraid that the refugees would bring Colombia's violence and crime with them. Often, they would not give homes or jobs to the refugees.

Human trafficking is the illegal buying and selling of people as **forced laborers**, soldiers, or slaves. Many Colombian refugees in host countries were afraid of being trafficked by guerrilla and paramilitary groups. These groups threatened the refugees. Sometimes they kidnapped young men and boys. They took them back to Colombia, where they were forced to work as soldiers.

Only about one in three Colombian refugees is given the chance to settle in their host country.

Colombia's Story in Numbers

During the 50-year-long conflict, more than

90,000

Colombians have disappeared.

Colombian refugees often avoided other refugees in their host country. They were afraid other refugees would tell the rebel groups where they were hiding. They often moved from place to place to avoid being found. Many dreamed of resettling farther away where they could truly feel safe.

The UNHCR gives refugees the basic rights of food, housing, jobs, and health care. HIAS is a Jewish organization from the United States. In Ecuador, it helps Colombian refugees find safety. Inside Colombia, the Norwegian Council of Refugees works with IDPs. It helps children get an education. It also helps Colombian refugees in Ecuador, Venezuela, and Panama gain refugee status.

Children have the right to live, play, and go to school without fear of being harmed.

Andres's Story: Struggles in Ibarra

At first, we were happy to be in Ecuador. We stayed in a tiny, one-room apartment while Papá looked for a place to live. Some people who were helping refugees gave us mattresses, blankets, and food for Mamá to cook with. They were kind to us.

But not everyone in Ecuador was friendly. When my parents visited apartments to rent, they were told they were no longer available. One apartment manager said to them, "We do not rent to Colombians." It took many weeks for Papá to find someone who would rent us a place to live.

It takes courage and hard work to start a new life far from your homeland.

Colombian refugees can go to school in Ecuador, but they often face discrimination.

My papá looked for work in many places. Once he was offered a job. Then, the boss looked at his papers and said, "You are Colombian? No, sorry." Finally, he got a job as a dishwasher in a restaurant. At school, I was beaten up by my classmates. "Go home to your country," they shouted at me. I often cried at breakfast and begged Mamá to keep me at home. At least I have some family around me.

Mamá and Papá watch the news about Colombia. They hope we can return to our village when our country is safe. Hopefully, we will find Diego waiting for us.

Hope for the Future?

The Colombian government wanted to bring peace to the country. It **negotiated** with FARC to stop the fighting. In 2016, both sides signed a peace deal. The deal means that poor farmers will be given farmland, and FARC will have a role in making decisions with the government about the country. In exchange, FARC agreed to hand in its weapons. In June 2017, the UN stated that nearly all FARC weapons had been collected.

Years of violence by FARC have made Colombians angry and suspicious. They are worried that FARC will not follow the rules of the peace deal. Many do not want the FARC guerillas to go free, because those soldiers hurt their families. Under the peace deal, the government promised **amnesty** to all guerillas who gave up their weapons.

Here, Colombian protestors against the war gather in Bolívar Square in Bogotá.

More than

250,000

Colombians have died in the civil war.

As peace comes to Colombia, many Colombians are still afraid to go home. Others have decided to return. They want to begin a new life, and they are hopeful for a new future for Colombia and its people. In 2016, President Juan Manuel Santos received an international award called the Nobel Peace Prize for his role in ending his country's long conflict.

President Santos has worked hard to bring peace to his country.

You Can Help!

In a world where we are all connected, it is important to be a global citizen. A global citizen is someone who helps make the world a better place. This can be done through actions and words. There are many things you can do to help welcome refugees to your community.

 Share with your friends what you have learned in this book. Encourage them to learn more about newcomers and refugees.

 Share a meal with a refugee family. Learn about the foods they eat.

 Reach out to a refugee in your community or school to offer friendship and support.

 Learn a few words of Spanish to make newcomers feel welcome. *Bienvenido* means "welcome." *Hola* means "hello."

 Take part in World Refugee Day every June 20.

 At home, at school, and in your community, learn to work out differences of opinion with respect and patience.

UN Rights of the Child

Every child has the right to practice their own culture, language, and religion.

You can help a refugee or newcomer feel welcome at school by offering your friendship and support.

Discussion Prompts

1. Explain the difference between a refugee, an immigrant, and an IDP.
2. What changes will the peace deal bring to Colombia?
3. Why is it important to be a global citizen?

Glossary

amnesty A legal decision that allows a person to go free without any punishment for their crime

civil war A war between groups of people in the same country

democracy A form of government in which people vote for the leaders who represent them

discrimination The unfair treatment of someone based on their gender, race, religion, or other identifiers

drugs Chemicals that affect your body

exploitation To take unfair advantage of someone

forced laborers People who are forced to work in unsafe conditions or for little pay

guerillas Groups of soldiers that do not belong to a regular government army

homeland The country where someone was born or grew up

host country A country that offers to give refugees a home

immigrants People who leave one country to live in another

independent Free from outside control

internally displaced persons (IDPs) People who are forced from their homes during a conflict, but remain in their country

negotiations Formal discussions between people who want to reach an agreement

quarry A place from which stones or other materials are extracted

rebel A person who fights against the government of a country

recruited Convinced to join a group

refugees People who flee from their own country to another due to unsafe conditions

resources A country's source of wealth, such as minerals

slums Parts of a city that are in bad condition, where poor people live

United Nations (UN) An international organization that promotes peace between countries and helps refugees

United Nations High Commissioner for Refugees (UNHCR) A program that protects and supports refugees everywhere

vulnerable At a risk of harm

Learning More

Books

National Geographic. *Every Human Has Rights: A Photographic Declaration for Kids.* National Geographic Children's Books, 2008.

Serres, Alain. *I Have the Right to Be a Child.* Groundwood Books, 2012.

Smith, David J. *If the World Were a Village.* Kids Can Press, 2011.

Wilson, Janet. *Our Rights: How Kids are Changing the World.* Second Story Press, 2013.

Websites

www.dltk-kids.com/world/colombia/index.htm
Find out more about Colombia, try some of the crafts and activities, and learn to count in Spanish.

www.ducksters.com/geography/country.php?country=Colombia
Discover more of Colombia's history and geography.

http://teacher.scholastic.com/activities/globaltrek/destinations/colombia.htm
Learn more about Colombia's history, culture, and famous writers and musicians from Colombia.

www.unicef.org/rightsite/files/uncrcchilldfriendlylanguage.pdf
Explore all of the rights protected by the UN Convention on the Rights of the Child.

Index

About the Author

Linda Barghoorn studied languages in university because she wanted to travel the world. She has visited 56 countries, taking photographs and learning about different people and cultures. Her father came to Canada as a German immigrant more than 50 years ago. Linda has written 11 children's books and is writing a novel about her father's life.